Edwin Doak Mead

The Roman Catholic Church and the School Question

Edwin Doak Mead

The Roman Catholic Church and the School Question

ISBN/EAN: 9783337022181

Printed in Europe, USA, Canada, Australia, Japan

Cover: Foto ©Suzi / pixelio.de

More available books at **www.hansebooks.com**

The Roman Catholic Church
and the School Question.

By EDWIN D. MEAD.

BOSTON : GEORGE H. ELLIS.

1888.

Price, Fifteen Cents.

The Roman Catholic Church and the School Question.

WHEN the foolish are hot, it is time for the wise to be cool. Eternal vigilance is the price of liberty, but a habit of viewing each midsummer explosion as the crack of doom is not the best qualification for the vigilance committee in the time of real danger. I trust I shall never be accused of political indifferentism; but sometimes in these heated weeks I count it expedient to say to some of my good friends, Republican friends and Democratic friends, that the present election seems to me the least important presidential election in our history, and that I think it makes very little difference whether Mr. Cleveland or Mr. Harrison be elected. There is no question in the country more important than the school question. There is no institution in the country, to my thinking, so important as the public school, none whose interests we should guard so vigilantly or so jealously. There is nothing in the country of which I am more jealous than the multiplication of Roman Catholic parochial schools. They will never give anything but a parochial education, never a catholic and broad education, and the system is bad. I am jealous of the constant unfair and captious fault-finding with the public schools in large Roman Catholic circles, and the manifest disposition to multiply criticisms and controversies and make trouble, out of which grist shall somehow come to the parochial mill. In the general interests of science and freedom and progress, I have more criticism to make upon the Roman Catholic Church than upon any other of our churches. But much more jealous than I am of parochial schools, or of Catholic opposition to the public schools, or of any Roman Catholic dogmas or aims or methods, am I that Catholic captiousness and unfairness, where they exist, shall not be met with feverish unfairness, but with justice and more than justice — with magnanimity. Arnold of Rugby used to say that the measure of his love for any institution was the measure of his desire to reform it. The measure of my love for any institution is always the measure of my resolution to defend it fairly and only fairly, and of my resentment of mere violent, blind abuse of its enemies or its critics. And it is because my devotion to the American public school is so sincere and so earnest, that I wish to express the hope, as a preface to such critical words as I shall have to speak, that there is not rife in this gathering, or in the association under whose auspices we here come together, anything of that spirit of wholesale, indiscriminate and wild denunciation of the Roman Catholic Church, which has characterized many recent meetings in Boston. However it may be with some of our Protestant clergymen, I trust that there is no woman in this league or in Boston who is bothered by the fear, which bothers one of our Protestant clergymen, that Archbishop Williams is fitting up some dungeons under the new cathedral. I trust there is no woman and no man here present who did not read with indignation and with shame the charge of one of our university professors to one of our large congregations last Sunday, that "Protestant men and women who have Catholic servants in their employ should say to them on the eve of election day that if they intended to vote at the dictation of the priests they must look for work elsewhere.' You know what that means. It means the discharge of the man or the woman who don't vote as we do. It means the boycott and the inquisition. The man who talks thus in a time like this abdicates the function of the scholar and advertises himself an unsafe public guide. No Catholic word has been so bad as this. No Catholic word has been so bad as the utterances from the platform of Music Hall last Sunday by the Protestant clergyman whose fulminations there we have become used to. I refer to this, a fair sample of numberless such utterances, simply because I think some of you may not know the pass to which this discussion has come. "The Mass a Roaring Farce" was the reverend gentleman's last Sunday subject, and this interesting episode is reported :

"He took from an envelope a little wafer, like those used in the Catholic Church, remarking that the communicant was not allowed to touch the wine cup, this being retained by the priest, who after the service generally got drunk on what was left. Romanists say that these wafers are the real Christ — these little bits of cracker, which are easily broken, that become lost, that fall in the mud, that are eaten by rats. If, as is claimed, each one of these wafers is Jesus Christ, then there are a hundred thousand Jesus Christs all over the known universe. There is no power in them, shouted the impassioned doctor, as he came to the edge of the platform and bent his body until his head almost touched his knees. If there were, I could not say these things against them. To show you it has no power, I will roll it over and break it."

And we read that the great audience of three thousand people, presumably all Protestant people, citizens of this "Athens of America," presumably graduates of our public schools; here broke into the wildest kind of applause, which lasted fully a minute and started afresh whenever the doctor attempted to resume his remarks. I do not know, ladies and gentlemen, what some of you may think of a spectacle like this in Boston ; I do not think it edifying. It is told of Dr. Johnson that when somebody expounded Berkeley's idealism to him, he brought his big cane or his heavy foot down solidly upon the earth and declared that thus he refuted it ; and he has imitators in this method of dealing with metaphysical questions, to this day. But Dr. Johnson would never have got through the freshman year in a theological school without knowing that such a representation of the doctrine of the real presence or of transubstantiation as that here reported is as untrue — the doctrine, when truly stated, is to the minds of most of us a gross error — as the method of representation is vulgar and offensive. Equally offensive and untrue are the representations of the Catholic Church and the Pope of Rome as the targets for sundry very uncomplimentary epithets from certain Old and New Testament prophets — epithets which have been bandied about not a little by some of our Protestant clergymen in this summer's discussions about the schools. I read a speech by one of our clergymen, at one of the Faneuil Hall or Tremont Temple meetings, which was largely devoted to arguing that the book of Revelation and even the book of Daniel denounce the Pope of Rome; and last Sunday another announced that the "mystery of iniquity" and "that Wicked," spoken of by St. Paul, in Second Thessalonians, was none other than this same Pope of Rome — evidently overlooking the apostle's remark that the said mystery of iniquity "doth already work." Now most of us hate to have a case against us "clinched with Scripture," most of us having a very high regard for the apostles and prophets and desiring to stand well with them. Appeals to the Bible therefore against our adversaries had generally better be as few as possible. So far as the Roman Catholic Church and the Pope are concerned, no thought of either ever entered the head of any Bible writer; the notion that there could have is ridiculous. When you hear any ingenious Protestant clergyman going back to Daniel or Second Thessalonians or the Apocalypse for arguments on the question of parochial schools or of the Boston School Board, I would suggest that you urge him, for the sake of economy in time, to skip that part of his talk.

And we have heard altogether too much in these days about the impossibility of a man being at once a good Catholic and a good American. The answer to such charges is the vast number of sincere and earnest Catholics who are among our most useful, faithful and loyal citizens. If we remember the doctrine of papal infallibility and the papal assertion of the supremacy of the church to the state, and if we press the logic of creeds and definitions to the extreme, we certainly come to a dilemma which the thoughtful Roman Catholic would do well to meditate upon. I fully endorse the conclusions of Mr. Gladstone, in his pamphlet on the Vatican Decrees, even to where he says that "no one can become the convert of Rome without renouncing his moral and mental freedom and placing his civil loyalty and duty at the mercy of another." This, I say, is the ultimate logic of the doctrine of papal infallibility and of ecclesiastical supremacy. But there is not a single church in the Evangelical Alliance which was represented in the recent remonstrance before the School Board which can abide the logic of its creed. "John Ward" was a Presbyterian who carried his creed into life with the honest relentlessness of the syllogism. I respect John Ward as much as I pity him and hate his creed and its logic. But many who are pledged to his creed do not hesitate to declare his course inhuman, in my ears; and sure it is that if the men who hold his creed should begin to live it out with inexorable logic, Boston would soon become a much worse place to live in than it is ever likely to become as the result of the Roman Catholic doctrine about church and state, to the ultimate logical issues of which doctrine so many of our Protestant clergymen are now endeavoring to crowd their simple Catholic neighbors. If a man did logically and absolutely appropriate the Calvinistic doctrines of total depravity, predestination and the eternal damnation of the majority, which are the nominal and standard doctrines of half the churches belonging to the Evangelical Alliance, I should say that he was an immoral, an inhuman and an irreligious man if he allowed himself to marry the woman he loves and become the father of children. But as matter of fact almost no Calvinist does or ever did hold those doctrines in their naked and logical severity. They are always modified and complemented in life and in thought by other doctrines, often held all unconsciously, by other great imperatives and truths of human nature and currents from the nature of things; and it would never occur to me to say, unless in scholastic disputation, that my neighbor could not be at the same time an honest Presbyterian and a good man. The radical had better not tell his Baptist or Methodist brother too often that he "renounces his mental freedom" when he subscribes to the doctrine of the infallibility of the Bible, as truly as his Catholic brother who accepts the infallibility of the Pope. If the writer of Genesis could make no mistake, why may not Leo XIII also be miraculously shielded? Personally I should expect his

History of the Middle Ages, which is about to be published, to be quite as free from errors as the Jewish books of Judges and Kings. As matter of fact, we know very well that the men who hold the doctrine of the miraculous inspiration of Genesis keep modifying the doctrine so that it shall not bring them into too sharp collision with Kensington and Berlin. And so the deliverances of papal infallibility will always be trimmed or explained away by the common sense of the faithful, whenever sufficiently serious exigencies require. Your Baptist brother, my good friend, cannot, I say, abide extreme and merciless logic; but you will not tell him carelessly that he cannot be a good Baptist and a truthful man. There is scarcely an Episcopalian, clerical or lay, in the circle of my personal acquaintance, who does not tell me that he does not believe in everlasting damnation; yet all pray to be delivered from everlasting damnation at least once a week, doubtless with the feeling of the old lady who preferred to bow at the mention of the Devil in the service — she "thought it was safer." There is scarcely a month that I do not hear some Unitarian minister approaching the mercy-seat "through Jesus Christ" or asking sundry benefits "for Christ's sake." It is habit, tradition, survival. They have no right to these phrases and will frankly tell you, if you ask questions, that they do not accept the doctrine which the phrases unquestionably imply. These practices are certainly very illogical, strictly speaking they are morally indefensible and bad! Yet it would not be right to tell your Unitarian or Episcopal brother of this sort, on the rough, common ground of life, that he is an immoral and a bad man. Do not then, in rough, practical matters, approach your Catholic brother as you have been doing. Neither strict logic nor lack of it settles these questions. When it comes to strict theological discussion, I am as ready to take a hand as anybody, whether it be with the Catholic or the Protestant; but on the plane where we are I protest against this vast amount of talk about the impossibility of Roman Catholics being good citizens. Nothing in the world can be so offensive to an honorable and patriotic man. The appeal is to facts. We are surrounded by good Catholic citi zens. Our regiments in the Civil War were full of good Catholic citizens. The late commander of our army, the hero whom we have just laid to rest, was a good Catholic citizen. One of our Protestant orators, with his pistareen logic about ecclesiastical supremacy, has just been saying that if Sheridan, on his ride from Winchester, had been met by his priest and ordered back, he would have had to turn back and would have turned back. I will tell you what Sheridan would have done. He would have said, "Go to the devil" — that is all. The battle fought and the rebels routed, he might have given ten minutes to the priest, time enough — no more — to give him a safe conduct through the lines and make an appointment for the discussion of ecclesiastical supremacy in the leisure of some summer after the war was ended.

The logic of duty, friends, the dictate of clear truth and justice, of humanity and of honor, is much more imperative and pervasive and reliable, is a much longer logic, than the logic of any Vatican decree, of the Thirty-nine Articles, or of the Westminster Catechism. This is not a good year to say that the Catholic cannot be a good citizen. This is the third centennial of the defeat of the Spanish Armada. The power of the Pope and the fear of the Pope in 1588 were ten times as great as they are today. The jealousy and hatred between Catholic and Protestant, the one or the other still sent to the stake or the gallows, according as the one or the other was in power, were ten times as great in England then as now. It was the year after every Catholic feeling had been inflamed by the execution of Mary Stuart. Probably half England still loved the old church best. Yet when the Spanish Armada, under the special benediction of the Pope, its aim the restoration of the Catholic power in the north of Europe, Elizabeth excommunicated and her subjects declared released from obligations, — when the Spanish Armada came bearing down on England, what Englishman forgot that he was first an Englishman, what Englishman asked whether he was Catholic or Protestant, as he hurried to the camp at Tilbury or until the wreck of the Armada strewed the seas? So it will be always.

Let America once really be in any danger from any Catholic power, and every healthy Catholic in Boston would rush to the recruiting office, snapping his fingers at every papal benediction and every papal anathema that could be read to him. The Catholic today has great respect for the Pope in his place, but if from now on he ventures to meddle unpleasantly with politics, he will be told very sharply, as Ireland has just been telling him, to attend to his own proper offices. So it will be with parochial schools. They will not continue permanently at all. They will continue and will multiply for a time if they succeed in convincing the people that they give a really good education, as good an education as the public schools. But if they do not give a sound, broad and liberal education but a sectarian, sickly, narrow education, and if this appears to the people, as it will be made to appear if it is the case, then all the encyclicals that can be written cannot bolster them up here in America in this nineteenth century. Every sensible Catholic will see the nonsense of it. He will see that his children will not be qualified to enter this great American life and to succeed in it. He knows too well what the institutions of this country have done for him and for his children, to allow any wool to be pulled over his eyes permanently, to serve any ecclesiastical interests. He will not long continue to hand over his money to build parochial schools, when he can send his children to the better public schools for nothing, without exceedingly solid reasons for it, much better reasons than have yet been given. There will be complaints, there will be revolts, then there will be compromises, and the parochial schools will fade away. A competent Irish authority has just told us, what I believe to be unquestionably the truth, that "if a vote of the Irish-Americans of Massachusetts, especially Boston, was taken nine tenths would give the public schools the first place." The parochial school is being forced upon the people by the priesthood. The mass of the Catholic people do not want it and do not like it. They will like it less and less every day, and, if we are fair with them, they will not long have it; their clerics will not face the results of too serious a collision.

If any of you are in doubt about the patriotism of your Roman Catholic brethren, you have only to examine the text-books — the histories, the reading-books — used in the parochial schools. Whatever criticism is to be passed upon some of these books — and I have a good deal to say about them presently — the lack of the patriotic element in them cannot be recorded. Many of these books ring with patriotism. The reading-books are as full of patriotic selections as most of the reading-books used in the public schools. They ring too with the spirit of democracy. The history of Ireland for these two long centuries, and the character of the institutions from which most of the Catholic emigrants to America have escaped, have not been such as to make any of them very enthusiastic for monarchies and aristocracies ; and they are not enthusiastic and do not teach their children to be. However much "divine right" of bishops there may be in the books, there is no "divine right" of kings. There is much sharp condemnation of tyrannies, much warm approbation of free institutions. Towards this American republic there is especially a feeling of gratitude for a toleration such as Roman Catholics have enjoyed in no Protestant country in Europe. There are pretty constant reminders of the intolerance and the disabilities under which Catholics have suffered in the Protestant world for the last two centuries. And is it to be wondered at? When we reflect upon it, it is a sorry history. The whole Jewish race has been dubbed deicides and treated as deicides for eighteen centuries, because some bigots among them eighteen centuries ago chanced to do what the Christian church has been pretty busy doing from that time to this — turned over to the executioner a heretic who disturbed the peace of Israel. The great mass of the people heard him gladly, and the priests were afraid to have him arrested openly for fear of the people ; yet the whole race has to suffer for it. And the whole body of Roman Catholics in Protestant countries for two centuries have been despised and called by every bad name that could be invented by Protestant ingenuity or raked out of the book of Revelation, been denied almost every political and social privilege, treated as mere hangers-on in the world, beings existing on sufferance, creatures of hardly the same blood as the Protestant — all in perpetuation of the exceeding great rage, the well warranted and wholesome rage be it said, of our Protestant fathers at the corruptions of the sixteenth century. Look no farther than England. Few liberal historical scholars will deny the political necessities for much of the anti-Catholic legislation in England from the time of Elizabeth to the time of William of Orange, when the lines that defined political and religious parties were so essentially the same. Yet I cannot read the very Bill of Rights without a blush; and the disabilities and oppressions of the Catholics of England and Ireland down almost to our own time constitute one of the most shameful pages in history. Do you say that these wrongs were more political than religious? You have no right to say it until you are ready to say the same of the Inquisition in Spain. About which same Inquisition, damnable enough surely in any case, very extraordinary misconceptions obtain. It is not at all uncommon to meet with the notion that the business of the Inquisition in Spain under Torquemada was to burn Protestants, although Torquemada was dead before there ever was a Protestant and while Luther himself was yet a boy. There may even be some here who would be surprised to learn exactly what prompted Ferdinand in his employment of the Inquisition and of the attitude of Pope Sixtus in the matter.

Before passing from the question of the political disabilities of Catholics in Protestant States, I should like to call attention to the statement which I find repeated in more than one of the Catholic geographies, that in the State of New Hampshire Catholics are still disqualified from holding certain offices. Can it be possible that this is the truth?

In the whole matter of toleration, Protestantism has no better record than the old church. It has simply been the Ins persecuting the Outs — one way in England and Germany, another way in Italy and Spain. Elizabeth's High Commission was only a Protestant Inquisition, and Archbishop Laud was no more tolerant than Torquemada or Catherine de Medici. The

New England Congregationalist will remember that it was not under Mary but under Elizabeth that Copping and Thacker and Penry and Barrowe and Greenwood were hanged, and by James I that our Pilgrim Fathers were "harried out of England." Toleration is not a tenet for which any church is to be thanked. It is a growth of civilization, which simultaneously affects all churches. Toleration is now popular, and I do not think it is likely ever again to become wholly unpopular. These Catholic reading-books are full of enthusiasm for it. These Catholic histories praise nobody quite so much, are quite so proud of nobody else, as Lord Baltimore, the Catholic founder of Maryland, the first American colony established on a basis of perfect tolerance; and they are quite as sincere in their praises of tolerance as some of our Boston Protestant ministers, and no more so. A century hence both parties will be much sincerer about it than they are today; and meantime it is wholesome and helpful that they should assume the virtue and praise it in their reading-books, even if they have it not. A century hence the Protestant party will say less about itself as the promoter of rational progress and inquiry, and the Catholic Church as the one great obstruction to science and the light. One of the Catholic members of the Boston School Board, as will be remembered, recently ventured to deny, in a communication to one of the newspapers, the truth of Mr. Swinton's statement, in his now famous little book, as to the Church's treatment of Galileo. But the facts are notorious; it is folly and fatuity to deny them. But there was nothing remarkable in this treatment of Galileo, nothing that the Catholic need apologize for to the Protestant. What this gentleman should have done was simply to remind the Protestant churches that they were tarred with the same stick. The opposition of the Church in Galileo's time to the teaching that the earth is round was just like the opposition of the Church in ours to the doctrine of evolution. Most of us younger men have been brought up on sermons on Christianity *versus* Darwinism; and until this very latest time, when the doctrine has so thoroughly established itself in the scientific world that loose condemnations of it have become ridiculous, the professor who ventured to talk evolution in the Protestant theological seminary was quite sure to be dealt with as summarily as Galileo was dealt with by Pope Urban and the Inquisition. Luther pronounced Copernicus's book, which he lived just long enough to read, damnable heresy. The Reformers generally ridiculed, despised and hated Copernicus, who was himself, as you well know, an honored canon in the Catholic Church, his name never anathematized by the Church. From that time to this, Protestantism has fought as surely and steadily as Catholicism every new idea in philosophy, in natural science and in Biblical criticism, which affected its orthodoxy, until the manifest absurdity of its positions compelled retreat and readjustment; and today St. George Mivart has a vastly easier time of it in the Catholic Church than Egbert Smyth at Andover or Professor Woodrow in South Carolina.

It will not be thought, after what I have said, that what I shall proceed to say upon the particular question which has arisen about text-books in our Boston schools, and about which we see this extraordinary excitement among our women, as well as among our men, is inspired by any unjust or unfair feelings toward the Roman Catholic Church. But it is not for this that I have asked your attention to these general considerations. I sincerely trust that I shall never be suspected of any unfair feeling toward any class in the community, and that it will never be necessary for me to give any pledge or proof of a just and impartial temper in dealing with any. I have dwelt upon these general points, because the particular quarrel into which we have been precipitated here in Boston has grown into a general quarrel, and we see the melancholy spectacle of a sort of religious war, Protestant against Catholic. The result is a mass of violent Protestant extravagance, misrepresentation, exaggeration and abuse much more discreditable than the three-column shriek from the Catholic priest in last week's Sunday *Herald* or than any Catholic word which has been spoken. This sort of thing we want to see eliminated from the present controversy. In an account of the work of Bishop England, of South Carolina, in one of these Catholic reading-books, the writer remarks:

" He soon discovered that the Americans, though bitterly prejudiced against Catholics, were yet disposed to be just and even generous. Their hatred of the Church arose from utterly false notions concerning her history and doctrines, and unfortunately the Catholics possessed no means of correcting these erroneous views. The press was in the hands of Protestants, who made use of it to disseminate the most injurious and absurd statements concerning the Church. The great majority of the people had never seen a priest, had never heard a Catholic sermon, had never entered a Catholic church, and had nothing to rely upon but the false traditions which they or their ancestors had brought from England."

I believe that this is still an accurate description of multitudes of American people. I hope that it is not a description of any Boston woman now preparing to vote on the school question. If any such is within the sound of my voice, I advise her to indulge in no general talk about the Roman Catholic Church until she has read at least one good book which authoritatively represents it, until she has read, if she can get nothing better, some of these histories and readers used in the Catholic schools. There is much to criticise in these books, but I think that nine Protestants out of ten will be chiefly surprised at the good that is in them.[1]

" The Americans," Bishop England found, "though bitterly prejudiced against Catholics, were yet disposed to be just and even generous." I believe the people of Boston are so disposed today, and to that justice and generosity I appeal and ask you to appeal. To stir that justice and generosity, against the hot and intemperate passion which has been ventilated in many quarters, is why I have here tried to emphasize the points on which the Protestant as Protestant has no right to throw stones at the Catholic, and some of the positive Catholic excellences and services which some are likely to forget. Were I engaged in an apology for the Catholic Church, I should go farther. I should enter the great domain of dogma, and declare on how many points I deem the Catholic doctrine superior to Protestant doctrine. I should tell you that the Catholic doctrine of purgatory, an intermediate state in which

[1] The Catholic text-books can all be found at Noonan & Co.'s, 17 Boylston Street, and probably at any of the Catholic bookstores.

men who are not great saints yet not great sinners are purified
and educated for the higher life, is to my thinking a better and
a truer doctrine than the sharp Protestant division of all men
into celestials and hellians, turned either to eternal beatitude or
eternal torment upon the accident of death. I should tell you
that the Catholic doctrine of miracle, a doctrine that asserts the
perennial power of God in the Church, as able to manifest itself
upon occasion at the hands of Ambrose and Francis or of the
pious Boston parish priest as at the hands of Peter and Paul
and Jesus and "them of old time," is a vastly nobler doctrine
than that of our Protestant churches, which recognizes a super-
annuated supernaturalism and no other. And I should tell you
that the Catholic doctrine of inspiration, the doctrine of a Holy
Ghost that is living and not dead, a divine spirit whose
authentic utterances are still to be heard among men and not
simply to be sought for in a book in the library, a Spirit not
local, historical, Palestinian, but throbbing, omnipresent, in the
Church of God — I should tell you, if you are Protestants, that
this doctrine is a sublimer and diviner doctrine than yours. I
am not, however, engaged in an apology for the Catholic
Church. I am here tonight chiefly to criticise it. Yet it is
only as you think upon these things, some of you who have no
thought upon them, only as you will do the Catholic Church
the justice to judge it by its ideals and its definitions, as well
as by its actual perversions, superstitions and narrownesses
that you will come to the present practical political questions in
the proper frame of mind, while they are mixed up, as they
have now unfortunately become mixed up in Boston, with a
general religious controversy.

I do not love the Roman Catholic Church. There is much
in it that I bitterly dislike and that I dread. I constantly find
it an obstruction in the way of causes which are dear to me. Its
general direction, its methods, philosophy, aim and atmosphere
are largely repugnant to my ideas. As some of you know, I
have spoken more sharply of its bigotries and superstitions
past and present, than I have ever spoken of almost anything
else — and I am pretty sure to speak sharply again. I am

always willing to be counted a member of a permanent vigilance committee charged with standing sentry on it. But I will also always stand sentry for it when it is unjustly besieged. I will never be privy to any assault on bigotry by bigotry. Bigotry is bigotry, whether Catholic or Protestant, and we want none of it. We want no religious crusade in the city of Boston. We want to hear no more talk about refusing to vote for this man for the School Board, or to approve that woman as a teacher in the public schools, simply because they are Roman Catholics, until the parochial school movement reaches a stage which in my opinion it is never going to reach. Whenever any decision or instruction goes so far as to compel any Roman Catholic father to withdraw his own children from the public schools, when he comes to think it a sin to send them there or to act as if it were a sin, then surely it will be a sin for him to have a hand in their administration, and his simple manhood will command him to withdraw from the School Board, if he belongs to it, and from the school-room, if he be a teacher. The public school must be in the hands of its friends. No man should be tolerated for a day in the administration of the public schools who is not a believer in them, no man who will not have his own children, if he has children, educated in the public schools and not in any private school, whether a Catholic parochial school at South Boston, an Episcopal parochial school in Brookline, or a private school on the Back Bay.

You are all quite familiar with the particular occasion of the present controversy. But all do not seem to be familiar with the actual words in Swinton's history which have led our school committee to throw that book out of the schools. So intelligent a paper as the Boston *Post*, in an editorial article only two days ago, a very admirable article in the main, referred to the passage as representing an indulgence as " a permission to commit sin." Such a reference as that at this late stage of a discussion which turns on careful definition does not do credit to that excellent newspaper. Much more discreditable is a reference to the note in the same words, in the recent report of the committee on text-books to the School

Board. What are the words of this famous passage? They occur, as most of you know, in connection with a brief general paragraph upon the German Reformation. We are told (p. 320) of the dissatisfaction and complaint which were prevalent at various practical abuses in the Church and at the claims of the popes to interfere in the affairs of the nations, of the resort of Leo X to an extensive sale of indulgences, which in former ages had been a source of large profits to the Church, to recruit his exhausted finances, and of how the offensive manner in which Tetzel, the agent for the sale of these indulgences in Germany, aroused the opposition of Luther, who, first having appealed to the Archbishop of Magdeburg to suppress the traffic, then made his appeal to the people by the publication of his famous ninety-five theses against indulgences, which precipitated the Reformation. And here is the explanatory note:

"These indulgences were, in the early ages of the Church, remissions of the penances imposed upon persons whose sins had brought scandal upon the community. But in process of time they were represented as actual pardons of guilt, and the purchaser of indulgence was said to be delivered from all his sins."

Well, I maintain that this note states the substantial truth of history. What does the text-book committee say in its recent report? It says that the teacher who used this text-book in the English High School appears to have taught that an indulgence "is a permission to commit sin;" and it continues — I quote its exact words: "This is not and never was true. It is true that it has been so represented, as the note affirms; but it should add when, where and by whom, and definitely. It certainly never was by any duly recognized authority in the Catholic Church."

I am not going to enter upon any discussion of the teacher in the High School. That subject is not now on the table, or, if it is, it is quite independent of the subject with which we are concerned. Mr. Swinton is not responsible for Mr. Travis. No author is responsible for the misconceptions or incompetence of any teacher. So far as particular points are concerned ten times as many mistakes, and ten times as harmful mis-

takes, are made every year by Massachusetts teachers about
the treatment of Quakers and Baptists by the early Massachusetts Puritans, about witchcraft, about the character of the
Plymouth and Boston colonies, as have ever been made about
indulgences and the causes of the Reformation. To urge, as
some have urged, that these should not be touched by a teacher
or by a text-book, for fear they will not be treated accurately, is
to bring us to a pretty pass. It is the author's right to pre-
suppose competent teachers; whenever any teacher proves himself incompetent, it is our right and duty to engage another.
It is the author's duty to tell the simple truth; if he does not
do this it is our duty to drop his book, and if he does do it it is
our duty to sustain him. The capital sin in education is to
accommodate ourselves to ignorance, whether on the part of
teachers or anybody else. On this policy of the presupposition
of incompetence, we shall presently have to leave John Rogers
out of the books, lest the boys and their teachers confound
him with the Sheffield cutler whose name is on their jack-knives.
I am quite ready to say, in a single word, that I think some of
Mr. Travis's illustrations, so far as I have examined the matter,
extravagant and misleading. I think he may justly have exposed himself to censure or to correction. He certainly did if
he spoke in the present tense and not the past, or if historically
he represented an indulgence as "a permission to commit sin."
As the committee says, this is not and never was true. But it is
not true that the note affirms, as the committee says it does, that
indulgences have been represented as "permissions to commit
sin." It says that they have been represented as "actual
pardons of guilt." "It should add," says the committee, "when,
where and by whom." Well, I suppose the author acted on
the presumption of brains. He is speaking of the abuses in
the sale of indulgences, which provoked Luther's protest. In
the early ages of the Church, he comments, indulgences had
been regarded in a certain way, but in process of time they had
become mischievously represented as pardons. The *when*,
clearly, is the time of Luther, the time which the author is
talking about; the *where* is the ground, at least, with which

Luther was acquainted; the *whom* are the venal churchmen against whom he rose — this is what the boy in the High School, with brains in his head, would understand the note to mean. It would never occur to the boy to think that the mis. chievous doctrine had been decreed and made orthodox by an œcumenical council, unless that notion was put into his head by an outsider. The mere phrase "in process of time" makes it perfectly clear that it was an abuse which had gradually grown up in the Church. It was certainly competent for the author to explain how long the process of time was, during which this corrupting representation of indulgences had been spreading in the Church; but whether the process was long or short affects no point involved in the controversy. If the abuse existed in Luther's time, which no man in his senses can deny, the book is vindicated. As matter of fact, the corruption had been spreading for two centuries. It prevailed in England in the time of Wyclif, a century and a half before Luther, and Huss rose against it in Bohemia. It prevailed in Spain and Portugal, in fact, at a time much nearer us than even the time of Luther.

"There is no greater heresy for a man," protested Wyclif, "than to believe that he is absolved from sin if he give money, or because a priest layeth his hand on his head and saith, 'I absolve thee; *for thou must be sorrowful in thy heart, else God does not absolve thee.*'" "It is plain to me," he said again, "that our prelates in granting indulgences do commonly blaspheme the wisdom of God, pretending in their avarice and folly that they understand what they really know not. They chatter on the subject of grace as if it were a thing to be bought and sold like an ass or an ox; by so doing they learn to make a merchandise of selling pardons, the devil having availed himself of an error in the schools to introduce after this manner heresies in morals."

These words of Wyclif's would have no meaning if this "selling pardons" were not rife all about him. The Prologue to the *Canterbury Tales* shows quite sufficiently that they were rife. Chaucer was Wyclif's contemporary, perhaps his friend, although Catholics claim that he was a good Catholic. Read his description of "the Pardoner," in the Prologue:

"His wallet lay before him in his lap,
Brimful of pardons come from Rome all hot," etc.

And Chaucer, who satirizes these corrupt " pardoners " as sharply as Wyclif himself does, lets us know that the whole country, "from Berwick unto Ware," was full of them. Must Chaucer and the poets follow the historians out of the schools? Wyclif's powerful *De Ecclesia* is full of indignant condemnation of the venal representations of indulgence by the English priests and bishops; and Huss, in his strong tractate against indulgences, used almost Wyclif's very words and almost the very words which Luther used after him. If any of you will read Loserth's learned work on *Wyclif and Huss*, and especially the chapter on the Controversies on Indulgences in Prague in the year 1412, you will almost think yourself reading the story of Tetzel and Luther at Wittenberg, so identical is the collision, so Tetzel-like the seller of indulgences with his drum and money-boxes, so Luther-like the great Bohemian Protestant. "All that I have thus far taught," Luther said himself, at the time of his excommunication, "I have learned from John Huss, but without knowing it." So gross was the abuse which was made of indulgences in Prague on the part of the Romish Curia, Loserth informs us, that "not only the friends but also the opponents of Huss were constrained to raise their voice." The King of Bohemia complained to the Pope that his dealers ' promise heaven to all that will yield up their gold." Huss himself says that Palecz, one of the pillars of the Church in Prague, admitted the palpable errors in the articles of indulgence. Of what sort were these errors? They could be of but one sort. They made the articles of indulgence, most perilous at best, appear till more completely "actual pardons for guilt." How did Huss enlist the sympathies of the bright students in the university, if he had no case? How did Luther so easily win and hold the ardent sympathies of the Wittenberg students, if he was simply manufacturing his charges against Tetzel and the Church?

But I think no member of our text-book committee would venture to deny the shameless abuse of indulgences in Germany in 1517. It is not necessary to go to a Protestant partisan, like D'Aubigné, for our history, although I am not impugning D'Aubigné. Go to Ranke, so impartial that he has been accused in Germany of writing history from a Catholic point of view. Ranke, says his Catholic French translator, 'guards and defends the church and its heads against unjust attacks and multiplied slanders, intelligently appreciates their position, their mission, and their duties. His *History of the Papacy* will do more for the cause of religion than Le Maistre's book, which has so many charms for the Catholic." Well, Ranke observes that the Reformation "may be said to have originated in the violent shock which Luther's religious feelings received from the sale of indulgences." But what was it in this that so shocked Luther? Ranke describes what it was in very short and sharp words — "the doctrine of a forgiveness of sins to be had for money." And Ranke, ladies and gentlemen, perhaps the most learned and impartial historian of our time — Ranke is a bad man to wrestle with. Read his chapter on the "Secularization of the Church," in his *History of the Papacy,* for the general setting of Luther's time. Then read his *German History in the Time of the Reformation* read simply the second book of the first volume, to let Ranke show you the frightfully mercenary interpretation of the doctrine of indulgence which had come about even before Tetzel's time, and then show you how Tetzel himself was — these are his own words — "the most shameless of all the commissioners." But how "shameless?" I ask again. It could be but in one way, I answer — by making the indulgences, most perilous at best, appear still more completely "actual pardons for guilt." Indulgences, like a multitude of the ceremonies and rules of the Church, were prostituted to mere money-making. Where was there a more zealous Catholic than Cardinal Ximenes? Yet even he in 1513 opposed the attempt to introduce the sale of indulgences into Spain; "for there was not a doubt in the mind of any reasonable man," says Ranke, "that all these demands were mere financial speculations."

But we do not have to depend upon second-hand information in this matter. Erasmus's *Praise of Folly* is in the libraries — and Erasmus was a Catholic. Ulrich von Hutton can

still be read. Luther's Ninety-five Theses are still extant.
Luther's letter to the Archbishop of Magdeburg, complaining
of the manner in which Tetzel and his associates were carrying
on "their scandalous traffic," as he describes it, is still extant.
Luther's sermon to his own people at Wittenberg, preached
weeks before he nailed his theses to the church door, is still
extant, and you may read the synopsis of it, not in the
Protestant D'Aubigné, but in the Catholic Audin :

"They say," he said, "that indulgences, applied to the soul that
suffers in purgatory, are imparted to it, and accounted for in the remission
of the sins for which it should still suffer." "If you have anything to
spare," he says again, "give it, in the Lord's name, for the building of St.
Peter's at Rome, but do not *purchase pardons*." "I complain bitterly," he
wrote to the archbishop, "of the fatal errors in which these men are involv-
ing the common people, men of weak understanding, whom, foolish as they
are, these men persuade that they will be sure of salvation if they only buy
their letters of plenary indulgence. They believe that souls will fly out of
purgatory the moment that the money paid for their redemption is thrown
into the preacher's bag, and that such virtue belongs to these indulgences
that there is no sin which the indulgences will not absolutely and at once
efface."

I could continue quoting such arraignments from Luther till
midnight. These arraignments of the mechanical, venal character of indulgences and of absolution at the time constitute
the whole sum and substance of his quarrel with the Church
at the beginning. They were prompted by the dangerous
errors into which he saw his own people were falling. They
were made on the very ground where the bad business was
going on ; made by a man who, intense and violent and often
coarse, was profoundly earnest and religious, not a careless and
irresponsible talker, but the most learned and powerful professor in the university ; and the justice and crying need of the
arraignments were instantly recognized by almost every
serious scholar in the university and every serious man in the
community. It was not with the doctrine of indulgence as
such that Luther quarreled at first, although afterwards he
attacked the whole system. In his very Ninety-five Theses he
said (see theses 71 and 72), "Cursed be whosoever speaks

against the Pope's indulgence . . . but blessed be he who opposes the foolish and reckless speeches of the preachers of indulgence." Even in the explanation which he published after his conversation with Miltitz, he still admits the doctrine of indulgences in a certain sense. As what less then could indulgences have been represented by clerics of the Tetzel sort, against whom Luther rose, than pardons, delivering their purchasers from the just penalties of sin? The whole commotion at Wittenberg has no meaning, the beginning of the Reformation has no explanation, unless the doctrine of indulgences was being represented and was being understood in the churches around Wittenberg substantially as " the doctrine of a forgiveness of sins to be had for money."

The text-book committee incorporates in its recent report a strict definition of an indulgence from a recognized Roman Catholic authority. That definition is correct. The following definition by our own Dr. Hedge is also correct, and it is more profitable for us to listen to, because it shows how easy is the corruption of the doctrine, a dangerous one at best, and the natural point of transition to those abuses which Ranke and Swinton and the various historians record and against which Wyclif and Huss and Luther rose in protest:

"Indulgence, according to the theory of the Church, was dispensation from the penance otherwise required for priestly absolution. It was not pretended that priestly absolution secured divine forgiveness and eternal salvation. It was absolution from temporal penalties due to the Church; but popular superstition identified the one with the other. Moreover, it was held that the supererogatory merits of Christ and the saints were available for the use of sinners. They constituted a treasury confided to the Church, whose saving virtue the head of the Church could dispense at discretion. In this case the application of that fund was measured by pecuniary equivalents. Christ had said, ' How hardly shall they that have riches enter the kingdom of heaven.' Leo said in effect, ' How easily may they that have riches enter the kingdom of heaven,' since they have the *quid pro quo*. For the poor it was not so easy; and this was one aspect of the case which stimulated the opposition of Luther. Penitence was nominally required of the sinner, but proofs of penitence were not exacted. Practically, the indulgence meant impunity for sin. A more complete travesty of the ospel — laughable if not so impious — could hardly be conceived. The

aithful themselves were shocked by the shameless realism which characterized the proclamations of the German commissioner, Tetzel." [1]

"Practically," says Dr. Hedge, "the indulgence meant
impunity for sin." The familiar story told by more than one
of the old German chroniclers, and passed on by the Lutheran
historians, has much the same significance, whether myth or
fact, as showing the short and natural logic of the common
man — the story of the Saxon gentleman who heard Tetzel at
Leipzig, and bargained with him for thirty crowns for a letter
of indulgence that should cover him in a revenge he meant to
take upon a man who had defrauded him. Armed with this,
the story goes, he, with his servants, presently fell upon Tetzel
in a wood between Jüterboch and Treblin, gave him a beating
and took away his chest; and Duke George, who appreciated
the situation, good-naturedly let him off for it. The terribly
mechanical aspect of the matter appears, the slight stress
which was laid upon the penitence part of the transaction,
in the fact that one could not only buy indulgences for
his own sins, but also for his friends in purgatory, who
were quite beyond the reach of his lowly and contrite heart
or of any spiritual influence of the Church. An indulgence,
if it does not free the soul from guilt, remits the punishment

---

[1] "The theory of indulgence may be said to resolve itself into the two
positions: (1) that, after the remission of the eternal punishment due for
sin, there remains due to the justice of God a certain amount of temporal
pain to be undergone, either before death in this world or after death in purgatory; (2) that this pain may be remitted by the application of the super-
abundant merits of Christ and of the saints out of the treasury of the Church,
the administration of which treasury is the prerogative of the hierarchy. It
must carefully be borne in mind that, in Roman Catholic orthodoxy, indulgence is never absolutely gratuitous, and that those only can in any circum-
stances validly receive it who are in full communion with the Church, and
have resorted to the sacrament of penance, in which alone, after due contrition and confession, provision is made for the remission of the graver penalty
of sin. The doctrine of indulgences, however, is singularly open to mis-
understanding; and in its practical applications it has too often been used to
sanction the most flagrant immorality. The scandalous abuses connected
with the 'pardoner's' trade, and in particular the reckless conduct of the
hawkers of the papal indulgence granted to those who should contribute
funds for the completion of St. Peter's, Rome, were, as is well known, very
prominent among the proximate causes of the Protestant Reformation." —
Encyclopædia Britannica, article on Indulgence.

"The plenary indulgence for all, the alleged object of which was to
contribute to the completion of the Vatican Basilica, restored the possessor

due for guilt. I speak now of indulgences according to their strict definition. And to most men forgiveness is simply escape from punishment. To be pardoned is to be let out of State prison. Orthodoxy unquestionably demanded penitence in connection with the granting of indulgence. But the abuse of the doctrine, the inevitable and indisputable abuse, brought about a state of things with reference to the punishments in purgatory to which a man's sins had justly exposed him like that which would obtain in Court Square if the judge could say to the moneyed thief, " I waive imprisonment for a thousand dollars, on condition of your sincere regrets." I wish to say just here that to my mind such a state of things does obtain to a great extent in the great inequality with which our system of fines applies to the poor and the rich — and some of the evils of it are very like some of the evils of indulgences. You will say that the sinner buying his indulgence knew that he was dealing with the divine powers, whose arms are very long, who

---

to the grace of God, and completely exempted him from the punishment of purgatory. But there were three other favors to be obtained by further contributions : the right of choosing a father confessor who could grant absolution in reserved cases, and commute vows which had been taken into other good works; participation in all prayers, fasts, pilgrimages, and whatever good works were performed in the church militant; lastly, the release of the souls of the departed out of purgatory. In order to obtain plenary indulgence, it was necessary not only to confess but to feel contrition ; the three others could be obtained without contrition or confession, by money alone. It is in this point of view that Columbus extols the worth of money; 'he who possesses it,' says he seriously, 'has the power of transporting souls into Paradise.' Never indeed was the union of secular objects with spiritual omnipotence more strikingly displayed than in this epoch. There is a fantastic sublimity and grandeur in this conception of the Church as a community comprehending heaven and earth, the living and the dead; in which all the penalties incurred by individuals were removed by the merit and the grace of the collective body. What a conception of the power and dignity of a human being is implied in the belief that the Pope could employ this accumulated treasure of merits in behalf of one or another at his pleasure! The doctrine that the power of the Pope extended to that intermediate state between heaven and earth, called purgatory, was the growth of modern times. The Pope appears in the character of the great dispenser of all punishment and all mercy. And this most poetical, sublime idea he now dragged in the dust for a miserable sum of money, which he applied to the political or domestic wants of the moment. Mountebank itinerant commissioners, who were very fond of reckoning how much they had already raised for the papal court, while they retained a considerable portion of it for themselves, out stripped their powers with blasphemous eloquence. They thought themselves armed against every attack, so long as they could menace their opponents with the tremendous punishments of the Church."— *Ranke.*

look through all pretenses and disguises, and with whom it is not safe to juggle. Yes, you can say that. But the Wittenberg sinner did not say it, and the system did not encourage him to think it. Ultimate issues and the divine powers were a very long way off, and pretty thoroughly discounted by the great mass of intermediaries. It was a system of extreme vicariousness from top to bottom, and Tetzel's indulgences were its *reductio ad absurdum.* One form of the indulgence was that whereby a man paid so much for the intercessory efforts in his behalf of the saints and the general heavenly host, and with these intercessions your Wittenberg butcher and baker in 1517 felt extremely safe, attaching quite as high an efficacy to them as to a lowly and penitent heart. The prayer-books of the time are one index to the state of things. There are prayers to which an indulgence for 146 days, others to which one for 7,000 or 8,000 years, are attached. If a prayer was so efficacious, what might not the superstitious votary be encouraged to hope from thirty crowns?

Tetzel was unquestionably an extreme man, as bad perhaps as the system could produce; but him, and many who, if not as brazen in the traffic, were just as corrupt, it did produce and long sustain. Ultimately his own party was forced to abandon him. Miltitz, the papal nuncio, in 1518, after Luther's vigorous onslaughts had made the scandals notorious and roused Germany, censured Tetzel in the name of the Pope, pronouncing ' the most entire and distinct disapprobation of the scandalous proceedings of the venders of indulgence;" and his general opinion of him appears from the fact of his writing to Pfeffinger of " the lies and frauds of this Tetzel." The whole Catholic party began straightway to feel the force of Luther's unsparing exposures and to take steps to reform itself from within; but the tendencies of Tetzel's time must not for an instant be confounded, as many Catholic writers seek to confound them in the popular mind, with the direction of things at the Council of Trent, which latter was really mainly owing to the stern rebukes by men like Luther of the corruptions here considered. It should not excite surprise that the doctrine of indul-

gences had sunk to this low form in the common understanding
and in common usage, when we consider the general corruption
of the Church at the time. I could take up a dozen doctrines
and show you that they had sunk quite as low, when measured
either by the authoritative doctrinal definitions, by the practice
of the Catholic Church in earlier times, or by the practice of the
Church in Boston today. The corruption of the Church, both
in point of popular doctrine and in point of morals, was such as
the world never saw before nor since. I do not ask you to take
D'Aubigné's word for it. I do not ask you even to take Ranke's
word for it. Read the general accounts by the Catholic Audin
and his particular admission of the abuse of the indulgences
Read the words of Cardinal Julian, at the Council of Basle, or
the disorders among the German clergy. Most important of all
take the evidence of honest Pope Adrian VI, the successor of
Leo X, crowned in 1522, when Germany was all ablaze with
Lutheranism. At the diet of Nuremberg, summoned to dea
with Luther, this honest Dutch Pope Adrian declared roundly
through his legate, that

" these disorders had sprung from the sins of men, more especially from th
sins of priests and prelates. Even in the holy chair," said he, " man
horrible crimes have been committed. The contagious disease, spreadin
from the head to the members, from the Pope to lesser prelates, has spread
far and wide, so that scarcely any one is to be found who does right and
who is free from infection."

If any fact in history stands avouched, it is that the mos
mechanical and venal interpretation of the doctrine of indul
gence had become prevalent in the Church in 1517, and tha
this was the immediate occasion of the Lutheran Reformation
The Roman Catholic Church for two centuries before that tim
has a bad record. It is a desire that that bad record shall b
covered up, that it shall be kept as much as possible out o
sight and out of remembrance — this, and not any honest fea
that teachers in our Boston schools will be telling their boy
that Archbishop Williams or Leo XIII issues licenses to com
mit sin — which is the motive of the present Catholic oppositio
to Mr. Swinton's history. We all of us, ladies and gentlemen

have a rather mixed and impure religious pedigree. We have all at times, I fear, been miserable sinners. Church of England people cannot be very proud of Henry VIII, of sundry proceedings on the part of Archbishop Whitgift, of the general moral condition of the Church at the time of the Wesleyan revival, of the system of church " livings," of the fact that a lot of their bishops today derive large revenues from the rents of grog-shops, of the perversions and extravagances of doctrine which have obtained and obtain today in large sections of the Church. The New England Congregationalist is not proud of the dealings with Quakers and Baptists and witches on the part of his ancestors, though his ancestors were no worse in this than other people at the time. The Boston Unitarian is not very proud, I take it, of the attitude of his father toward Emerson and Theodore Parker. But the Roman Catholic is haunted to a much greater extent than other people by the hobgoblin of consistency. His whole theory of his miraculously inspired and guided and shielded church compels an excessive anxiety to show a good record. But, ladies and gentlemen, the record is very streaked and speckled. The record is blackest at the time when Luther was born in Germany. Among the abuses of that time none was more flagrant than the utterly mechanical and venal ideas of indulgences which were encouraged and which prevailed among the clergy and among the people. We are not teaching our children honest history, we are not showing them the justification or the explanation of one of the greatest movements in history, of the very central and most influential movement in all modern history, if we blot that fact from their books. In consenting to remove Swinton's text-book from our public schools, the School Board of the City of Boston has allowed itself to serve the interests of ignorance, of narrow prejudice, and of a restive, thin-skinned, finikin sectarianism. I say nothing of motives — I know well what good motives and what conscientious care there have been on the part of men whose conclusions I do not approve — but this, I say, is how history will record the fact. And history will remember that when this test-case was thus settled by the votes of fourteen men — 10 Catholics, 3 Protestants, 1 Jew — there stood up in protest two women. I do not say they knew more than these others, I do not say they were more conscientious, I do not say they had thought more about the matter; but I say history will remember that there stood up in protest these two women.

The text-book committee inform us, ladies and gentlemen, that before Swinton's history was dropped from the schools, the attention of the publishers was called to the defective character of the note, and imply that if the note could have been properly corrected the book would have been retained. I should like to know how serious an effort was made to this end. I should like to know what correction the committee would have deemed proper. I venture to say that if the publishers of the book can be shown tomorrow that there is any real likelihood of the note being understood in the schools as referring to today and not to the sixteenth century, any likelihood of its being understood to relate to any doctrinal standard or to present practice, the note will be expanded instantly. But I also venture to say that the more the note is expanded in fidelity to the truth of history, the more explicit the account is made of the abuses which provoked the Reformation, the more the book will be condemned by those who instigated the present opposition.[1]

---

[1] On the day on which I spoke (Oct. 1) there appeared a communication in the Boston *Herald*, which I had not read, from a prominent member of the School Board, Mr. E. C. Carrigan, containing information of very great significance upon this point. Mr. Carrigan is a man with Irish blood in his veins, and has expressed very warm and very proper resentment at the deluge of indiscriminate denunciation which has been poured out upon "Irish Catholics" by Protestant orators in Boston this summer. Whether he is himself a Roman Catholic or not I do not know. At any rate, his traditions and affiliations give him exceptional opportunities to understand the Catholic position. What more concerns us here, he is an earnest and energetic supporter of the public school system. "The establishment of parochial schools in Massachusetts" he declares to be "a most serious mistake, if not a great misfortune, especially to those who attend them, and that schools wholly supported and controlled by the people are the best schools for the children of all the people." Nothing in the present torrent of abuse, he tells his fellow-citizens of Irish ancestry, should be allowed to weaken their faith or interest in the American common school, "wherein the children of all Irish parents have an equal chance with others to secure the greatest prize of life, an education which fits them for citizenship and to successfully compete in the great business and professional world." Speaking of

I should never have known, had not the present controversy prompted me to a critical examination, how excellent a book this little history of Swinton's is. I have been especially impressed by the impartiality and the rare tact with which the author steers through those stormy periods where Catholicism and Protestantism clashed — the time of the Huguenots and St. Bartholomew's, the time of Alva in the Netherlands, the religious persecutions, now Catholic, now Protestant, under Henry VIII and Mary and Elizabeth. I should like especially to speak of Swinton's warm recognition of the services of the Catholic Church during the Middle Ages. I should like to

Swinton's history, he says, " No topic of such importance as the Reformation, whether taught from a text-book or orally, should be presented other than fairly, fully, impartially, so that the student may have as clear and as intelligent understanding of this subject as others in general history, whether it displeases a priest, preacher, parson or other citizen." He shows conclusively, I think, exaggerations and errors on the part of the teacher in the High School; although his apology for the dropping of Swinton's text-book, "simply and solely because imperfect teaching resulted from its use," is certainly a very poor apology. Mr. Carrigan has probably had a larger experience in connection with the public schools, perhaps knows more personally about the public schools, than any other member of the present Boston School Board. And he is, as I have said, an energetic man. While the text-book committee was telling us that the publishers of Swinton's history refused to change the offending note about indulgences, Mr. Carrigan was in New York reading the page in a proposed new edition of the book, submitted to him by the publishers, in which the note is changed. And how changed? Here is the text of the new note, as he gives it:

" Indulgences were authorized by the councils of the Church as a remission of the temporal penances imposed for sins; and, in the theory of the Church, they always presupposed confession and repentance on the part of the sinner."

If it be true that the author and the publishers of the book have agreed to a change like this, omitting the reference to the abuses of the doctrine in the time of Luther, which was the one point of moment, they have done it to satisfy the Catholic demand. And if this is the Catholic demand, then what I have declared above is strictly confirmed — that the motive of the Catholic opposition to the book is simply the desire to cover up a bad chapter in the history of the Church, the desire that the children in the schools shall not learn that Luther had sufficient provocation and Protestantism its justification. The *theory* of the Church is not the question; the *practice* of the Church in the fifteenth and sixteenth centuries is the question. If the charge which I here make is not true, then let the Catholic opposition declare that the following note would satisfy them:

Indulgences, as authorized by the councils of the Church in early ages, were remissions of the temporal penances imposed for sins. In the theory of the Church, they presupposed confession and repentance on the part of the sinner: but in process of time they had become widely represented in the Church as actual pardons, and the purchaser of indulgence was said to be delivered from the punishment due for his sins. This gross abuse aroused Luther and thus brought on the Protestant Reformation.

quote his high tribute to the monasteries, which were the arks of learning and the centers of almost every civilizing influence left in those dark and troublous centuries succeeding the breaking up of the old Roman system. "The Church," he says, "was the bridge across the chaos, and linked the two periods of ancient and modern civilization."

I quote this passage for a special reason. It is for saying the same thing that one of the members of our school committee, Dr. Duryea, was held up to execration yesterday on the platform of Music Hall by the passionate Protestant whom I have once quoted. Dr. Duryea, as scarcely needs be said to this audience, was quite right. He was only saying what every scholar knows perfectly well, what not to know proclaims a man in so far uneducated. This passionate Protestant went farther. He circulated a petition, which he asked every man, woman and child to sign, urging Dr. Duryea, inasmuch as "he lacks either the intelligence necessary to formulate a correct opinion concerning indulgences as taught by popes and practiced by priests, or the honesty and bravery to tell the truth," to resign his place on the School Board and "give place to a better educated or more truth-loving man." Well, I think Dr. Duryea's conclusions regarding Mr. Swinton's book erroneous. He does not read history as I do, or he is affected by considerations which I know nothing of. But the opinion concerning indulgences talked of by the gentlemen at Music Hall was never taught by any pope with whose teachings I am acquainted ; and a resolution such as this of which we read is a disgrace to any man who talks of education and the love of truth. The acme of disgrace is reached when children are exhorted to enlist in this religious warfare.

There has been altogether too much arraignment of the motives of Rev. Dr. Duryea here in Boston in these last days, some of them in places where we have a right to expect better things than we expect from the platform of Music Hall. I have even heard him criticised for saying, what would seem to be obvious to the narrowest intelligence, that he felt his daughters to be safer in Boston for the sake of the Roman Catholic

Church. Do these critics realize what the Roman Catholics of Boston would be, if their religion and their Church were taken away from them tomorrow? There seems to be an agreement in some quarters, one is sometimes tempted to think, that nothing good and anything bad may be said of the Roman Catholic. Some of our clergy have recently set out to describe the personal immoralities of certain Roman Catholics in Boston. Without doubt a melancholy catalogue could be made. And a bad enough catalogue could be made of Baptist adulterers and Episcopal embezzlers and Universalist tipplers. Let us not make that catalogue this year. And let there be less hasty talk about men's motives in complex matters like the present. Let us deal with facts as clearly and sharply as we please, but let us leave each man's conscience to himself. If I felt sure that half of those who have to deal with this matter brought to it half the conscientiousness and half the open-mindedness of Dr. Duryea, I should be twice as hopeful as I am of the right issue.

How do our Catholic brethren treat Luther and the Reformation? What do they teach their children in their own schools? Well, here is one of their histories, a very popular one, by Gazeau.[1] Here the protest against indulgences and the outbreak of the Reformation are made to appear as the result of Luther's jealousy and indignation that the sale of indulgences was not intrusted to his order, the Augustinians, instead of to Tetzel and the Dominicans. He was angry and mortified too that the people deserted his pulpit and flocked to hear Tetzel. Gilmour and others similarly ascribe Luther's movement to his indignation and pique at the "slight" put upon him and the Augustinians in not being intrusted with Tetzel's office. Tetzel is praised by Gazeau as an eloquent and learned man, who responded to Luther with "a masterly defense," — which, as the author truly remarks, the students of Wittenberg burned in the university square. Why did they burn it? The reason assigned by our author is their dislike of "free speech." There

[1] *Modern History.* Adapted from the French of the Rev. P. F. Gazeau, S. J. New York: The Catholic Publication Society. 1887.

is not one word of condemnation of Tetzel and the abuse o
indulgences.   There is only praise for Tetzel, and his succes:
is declared to be a proof of "the faith and the devotion of th
people."   Luther is represented as an altogether unscrupulou:
and turbulent fellow.

> "Wicked men," says the author, "are always disposed to rebe
> against authority.   The sale of indulgences and the word 'reform' wer
> simply made the pretext by the able but unprincipled Luther for the ou
> burst of the storm that was to devastate Europe and break up the spiritua
> unity of Christendom."

The general religious condition of Europe, as here painted
at the time when Luther rose, is something very beautiful
almost idyllic.

> "Christian Europe was at peace, forming but one great family, numberin
> as many members as there were nations.   Notwithstanding dynastic trouble
> and national rivalries, all Christendom was united by one creed around
> common altar and in obedience to the same infallible spiritual authority
> the Vicar of Jesus Christ.   The head of the Church, venerated as th
> universal father of the faithful, sent zealous missionaries to the idolatrou
> races of the New World, while in Europe he exerted his influence t
> encourage learning and to mature Christian civilization."

It was surely a pity to break into that delightful calm with
pothering doctrine of justification by faith!   What was thi:
doctrine of "justification by faith?"   Why, it was a doctrine, we
learn, that, "provided men *believed* in Christ, it mattered littl
what they *did*," and thus "justified all evil actions."   And thi:
was specially dangerous "at a time when laxity of moral:
widely prevailed"—for it is admitted that abuses "certainly
existed," that the lives of many of the clergy were scandalous
and that the general state of morals was bad.   But why wa:
this?   And who shall blame anybody for any definition o
transubstantiation, after this definition of justification by faith:
Time forbids the citation of all the characterizations of Luthe
which follow, and which altogether could leave in the mind o
a boy or girl only the impression of some monster little removec
from Bluebeard.

> "The pretended reformer respected the laws of morality no more tha

those of justice." "To justify his enormities he said that he was inspired by heaven." "No one can peruse without a blush of shame and indignation the coarse jests, the buffoonery, and the indecencies with which his works are sullied." "It is difficult to conceive," concludes the author, "how such a leader could have found followers, were it not known what power passion, pride, money and pleasure have over the human heart." Protestantism spread rapidly because it "pandered to corrupt nature."

And this explains the success of Luther and the Reformation! And "it is very important," as our author says, "that students should have a clear conception and knowledge of the causes that led to this revolt." Ladies and gentlemen, do we want Mr. Swinton's note expanded in that direction? Does this satisfy Father Metcalf's scrupulous anxiety for exact historical truth?

Let me hasten to say that this is perhaps the worst of the histories which I have examined. But this is a very popular history, and others are almost as bad. It is not this which misrepresents Luther's marriage, or describes Calvin as a man expelled from the university on account of his immoralities, or John Knox as a "bad priest," or as "the ruffian of the Reformation."

These books by Fredet and by Spalding, popular books in the schools, give a far truer idea of the abuses which provoked the Reformation than does this other. As to the man Martin Luther, his defense among Catholic scholars may be left to the fine and fair minds of their own number, men like Stolberg and Schlegel. Stolberg, in his strictures upon Luther's doctrines, "would not cast a stone" at his person. "In Luther," he said, "I honor not alone one of the grandest spirits that has ever lived, but a great religiousness also, which never forsook him." This for scholars — but who shall protect the children? Luther was coarse — it was a coarse time; he did jest; there is buffoonery. But as these things here appear, they are not true; and here they should not be spoken of at all.

Here is a history — a *History of the World*, by John MacCarthy,[1] a book of the same scope as Swinton's, to

---

[1] *History of the World, for Schools and Colleges.* By John MacCarthy. New York: The Catholic Publication Society. 1887.

which I wish to pay almost unqualified praise. It admits many
things discreditable to Catholics, which Swinton passes. It
mentions the fact, which Swinton passes, that a *Te Deum* was
sung in Rome, by order of Pope Gregory XIII, in honor of the
Massacre of St. Bartholomew's, although it makes a lame
apology for it. Its account of Luther and the Reformation
is almost entirely admirable, intelligent, spirited and almost
wholly just, a vastly better account than that in the history
which I understand is probably to supersede Swinton in our
schools; I ask you to compare the two.[1] It is a book which I
would willingly and gladly place in the hands of my own boy,
if I had one. I do not think I could myself write a more
impartial book. An exceedingly good book too is Hassard's
History of the United States.[2]

I wish that I might enter upon a more searching examination here of the text-books used in the Catholic schools. I want
to have you understand just what kind of history the scrupulous
sticklers for exact truth who are troubled by Mr. Swinton do
approve, what kind of things they would have children think
have come about "in the process of time." I shall hope for
some early opportunity to bring this subject more fully before
our public, if not in another address, then in the newspapers.
These books are not without excellences, but on the whole the
examination of them has been a depressing business. There
is no book among them worse than this exceedingly popular
Bible History, with an appendix of Church History, by one of
the bishops of the Church, Bishop Gilmour of Cleveland,[3] a
book commended by the Pope, by Cardinal Manning, and by
almost every leading American dignitary; in fact, there is no
other book which prints so many or such imposing commenda-

---

[1] Anderson's notice of the Reformation is ridiculously timid and inadequate. Luther
and his protest are mentioned almost as a by-the-by under the reign of Charles V. No
account whatever is given of the subject of indulgences. Luther's Ninety-five Theses are
said to have been directed against "the doctrines of the Catholic Church," a most careless and
incorrect statement.

[2] *History of the United States of America, for the Use of Schools.* By John R. G.
Hassard. New York: The Catholic Publication Society. 1887.

[3] *Bible History, Containing the most Remarkable Events of the Old and New Testa-
ments To which is added a Compendium of Church History. For the Use of the Catholic
Schools in the United States.* By Right Reverend Richard Gilmour, D.D., Bishop of
Cleveland. New York, Cincinnati and Chicago: Benziger Brothers, Printers to the Holy
Apostolic See.

tions. It is a thoroughly bad book. I should like to read you much from it. I will read a single paragraph, from the close of the account of the reigns of the Tudors, in which the persecutions under Henry and Elizabeth are made so much of, and the vastly bloodier career of Mary is not mentioned. "To make converts," the author tells his young readers,

" Catholicity has ever appealed to reason ; Protestantism, like Mohammed-anism, to force and violence. In England and Scotland Protestantism was forced upon the people by fines, imprisonment and death ; in Germany and Prussia, Sweden and Denmark and Norway, the same. In America the Puritans acted in like manner."

Ladies and gentlemen, did you ever read the Edict of 1550, with which Alva went armed into the Netherlands? Let me read you a brief passage from it, for two reasons :

" No one," said the Edict, " shall print, write, copy, keep, conceal, sell, buy or give in churches, streets, or other places, any book or writing made by Martin Luther, John Ecolampadius, Ulrich Zwinglius, Martin Bucer, John Calvin, or other heretics reprobated by the Holy Church ; . . . nor break or otherwise injure the images of the Holy Virgin or canonized saints ; . . . nor in his house hold conventicles or illegal gatherings, or be present at any such in which the adherents of the above-mentioned heretics teach, baptize, and form conspiracies against the Holy Church and the general welfare. . . . Moreover, we forbid," continues the Edict, " all lay persons *to converse or dispute* concerning the Holy Scriptures, openly or secretly, especially on any doubtful or difficult matters, or *to read, teach, or expound the Scriptures*, unless they have duly studied theology and been approved by some renowned university ; . . . or to preach secretly or openly, or to *entertain* any of *the opinions* of the above-mentioned heretics ; . . . on pain, should any one be found to have contravened any of the points above mentioned, as perturbators of our state and of the general quiet to be punished in the following manner."

And how were they to be punished? The Edict went on to provide that such perturbators of the general quiet are to be executed, to wit : the men with the sword and the women to be buried alive, if they *do not* persist in their errors ; if they do persist in them, then they are to be executed with fire ; all their property in both cases being confiscated to the crown. The Edict further provided that any who failed to betray a suspected heretic, or who lodged or entertained any such, or furnished any with food, fire or clothing, should be liable to the same punishment as if suspected or convicted themselves. All who knew of any persons tainted with heresy were required to denounce them, on pain of severe punishment; and the most ignoble principle of human nature was appealed to in the further provision "that *the informer*, in case of conviction, should be entitled to one half the property of the accused, if not more than one hundred pounds Flemish; if more, then ten per cent of all such excess." Treachery to one's friends was encouraged by the provision, "that if any man, being present at any secret conventicle, shall afterwards come forward and betray his fellow-members of the congregation, he shall receive full pardon;" whereas it was ordered that if any person, of whatsoever condition, should ask for the pardon of any condemned heretic or present any petition in favor of any, or if any one having authority should grant any pardon or favor, he should be declared forever incapable of civil and military office, and be in danger of severe punishment besides.

You will say, perhaps, that Holy Church and Holy Philip did not really mean this. They meant to terrorize the Netherlands by hanging up this frightful proclamation, but it is against all conscience and all humanity that they should carry it out. My friends, during the six years of Alva's government in the Netherlands, his executioners put to death 18,000 persons, to say nothing of the victims in cities captured by his troops or the hosts that fell in battles.

I read this edict, I say, for two reasons: as an illustration of the Catholic "appeal to reason," as opposed to the Protestant methods of "violence and force;" and as being one of the things which the Catholic text-books "fail to state." "The manuals of geography hitherto used in our schools," says the preface of one of these geographies — and the manuals of geography are largely manuals of history — "are not only objectionable on account of their misstatements, but are still more objectionable and defective on account of what they suppress or fail to state." It is interesting to go through these books and observe what they "fail to state," and then observe some of the things to which they are able to give so much space. There is room to

state that Ireland " is noted," among many other things, "for
the unwavering fidelity of its people to the Catholic Faith ; " but
there is not room to state that the Netherlands are noted for
anything besides their "low situation, numerous canals and
windmills." There is room to speak of "many Catholics" ex-
iled to Siberia, but of nobody else ; to note that the States of
the Church are " at present usurped " by the King of Italy, but
to say almost nothing else about the whole history of Italy. A
primary object everywhere is to make these books for school
children serve the purposes of theological and sectarian controversy.

How about America? Here is Sadlier's smaller geogra
phy [1] — a very popular book in the parochial schools, and, like
the other books in the series, a beautiful book. It contains
probably all the history of the United States that some of the
younger and poorer children, who leave school early, ever
get. If they do get more, I could quickly show you that they
are quite likely to get what is worse. Let me read to you the
section devoted to the history of the United States (Lesson
xxxiii, p 22):

What can you say of the United States? — It is the most populous and
powerful country in America.

By whom was this country originally inhabited? — By the Indians.

By whom were the Indians dispossessed of their lands ? — By the
Spanish, English and French colonists.

Who were the first explorers of great portions of our country ? — Catholic missionaries.

Who discovered and explored the upper Mississippi? — Father Marquette, a Jesuit missionary.

Where, in many of the States, were the first settlements formed ?
— Around the humble cross that marked the site of a Catholic mission.

What political division is the United States ? — A republic.

How long has it been a republic? — One hundred years.

To what nation did the thirteen original States belong ? — To England.

When did they declare themselves independent ? — July 4th, 1776.

Why did they declare their independence ? — Because they were unjustly oppressed by England.

---

[1] *Sadlier's Excelsior Introduction to Geography*. Designed for Junior Classes. By
a Catholic Teacher. New York: William H. Sadlier. See also O'Shea's *Comprehensive
Geographies*. New York : P. O'Shea.

What is the war called which occurred at this time between the United States and England ? — The war of the Revolution.

What Catholic nation very materially assisted the Americans during this war? — France.

How long did the war of the Revolution last? — About eight years.

At its close, who became the first President of the United States — George Washington.

This is the whole lesson. This is the general account of the colonization and early history of the United States. And this is a good sample of the proportion of the role assigned to Jesuit missionaries all through these books. You have heard of the boy who once asked his father, who was forever telling of his tremendous exploits at Bull Run and Gettysburg and Cold Harbor, "Father, did anybody help you put down the rebellion?" The descendant of the New England Puritans or of other worthies, whom some of us have been in the habit of thinking as standing for something in this American enterprise, is moved to ask the Jesuit, when he reads of all his accomplishments, in these books, "Did anybody help you found the American republic?"

Under the special head of New England, in this particular geography, comes this further historical information, so admirably calculated to clear up anything left doubtful as to the genesis and significance of New England in particular:

What was the first settlement in the New England States? — A Jesuit mission on Mount Desert Island (in 1612).

By whom was this settlement destroyed? — By the English.

What people made a permanent settlement in Massachusetts in 1620 — The Pilgrim fathers.

Who were they? — English Protestants who, being persecuted by their Protestant fellow countrymen, took refuge in America.

How did they act in their new home? — They proved very intolerant and persecuted all who dared to worship God in a manner different from that which they had established.

That is all. The important, significant thing about the founding of New England is supposed to be told — there is no room for anything more than the leading facts. Now, ladies and gentlemen, you do not need to be told, and the makers of this book do not need to be told, that this is not history. History is not history at all save as its proportions are preserved. The Jesuit missionaries were heroic men and they are most interesting figures — we are glad that our own Mr. Parkman has written so much and so well about them. But their settlements and efforts were sporadic, and have had almost no influence upon the main currents of our American life and the development of our institutions, whose sources are here left almost unnoticed. The "Jesuit mission on Mount Desert Island" should not be mentioned in a primary text-book. It is questionable whether even Father Marquette should be mentioned in a book which has no space to tell how the present Northwest became what it is. The boy or girl who learns history from such books learns no history.

These geographies are stamped on the title-page as by a "Catholic teacher." Many of the books are marked as belonging to a "Catholic Educational Series." Here is the "Young Catholic's Fifth Reader," almost every portrait in it that of a bishop. This Third Reader, "in common with the other books of the Catholic National Series, has one chief characteristic," says the preface, "viz., a thoroughly Catholic tone, which will be found to pervade the whole book."[1] About that there is no doubt. From the first story, on "Bessie's First Mass," to the pieces on "How to be a Nun," "Saint Bridget" and "The Saint Patrick Penny," the "thoroughly Catholic tone" never fails. The Catholic name and atmosphere and effort are everywhere. Ladies and gentlemen, that is bad. My good Catholic friends, that is bad for you, bad for your children. It is not good for any of us to let our denominationalism be the "chief characteristic" of any of our books, much less of our children's books. We do not want, any of us, Catholic reading-books, nor Quaker spelling-books, nor Jewish geographies, nor Baptist histories, nor Presbyterian grammars, nor High Church cook-books nor Unitarian geologies, nor Trinitarian arithmetics. I have heard a story of a little girl who belonged to a Presbyterian

---

[1] *The Third Reader*. Catholic National Series. By Right Rev. Richard Gilmour, D.D., Bishop of Cleveland. New York: Benziger Bros.

family, coming home from school in some distress because one of her young Jewish friends had claimed that Jesus was a Jew. "Rachel says, mother, that Jesus was a Jew." "Yes, dear, Jesus was a Jew." "But how could he be a Jew, mother? Was he not the son of God, and isn't God a Presbyterian?" I wonder sometimes, when I note the sectarian atmosphere that prevades many homes, that God isn't thought to be a Presbyterian or a Baptist much oftener than he is. And our dangers will grow much graver than they are if we extend this sort of thing into our schools and set our boys and girls to studying Episcopal histories and Catholic geographies.

My good friends, we cannot afford, any of us, to live and breathe in these provincial atmospheres. You cannot afford, my Catholic brother, to let your boy grow up feeding on such history as I have said something of here tonight and as I may say more of at some other time. Defend your religion, in heaven's name, with all the vigor you will, and you may be very sure that nothing that is true and good in it has anything to fear. But do not so far wrong yourselves, do not so wrong your children, as to permit them to grow up prejudiced and jaundiced by such teachings as these. Let us at any rate have "free trade" in knowledge, or if "protection," then not protection by a Chinese wall bristling with vulgar misrepresentations of our neighbors, and thick and thin excuses and denials of all our own family faults.

My Catholic brother, are you doing your duty as a citizen of this free republic, are you doing your duty to your children, if you let them get their history from books in which every "stronghold of bigotry and intolerance" is always an anti-Catholic place? Is it right to let them be taught that "the Holy See has been God's instrument in conferring upon Europe all the real good she enjoys?" Is it right to teach them that "to Catholics are due nearly all the valuable inventions we have?" Is it right to teach them that "the only bond of unity among Protestants is a common hostility to Catholicity?" Is it right to teach them that the English free-thinkers from whom Rousseau and Voltaire drew some of the ideas which wrought the French Revolution were men who "denied the difference between good and evil?" Is it right to represent the Thirty Years' War as a Lutheran rebellion assisted by "the Protestants of France," saying no word of Cardinal Richelieu's hand in the matter? Is it well to harp so much on Salem witchcraft, and to say nothing of the 600 condemned in one district in France by Boguet, of the 50 who suffered at Donay, of the fact that the "witches' hammer" — one of the "inventions" not catalogued by Bishop Gilmour — was the work of two German Dominicans? Is it right to record the reported answer of the Duke of Guise to his Huguenot would-be assassin, " If your religion teaches you to assassinate me, mine obliges me to pardon you," and to fail even to mention the assassination of William the Silent by the paltry wretch, Gérard, an assassin fortified for his task by "holy communion," and applauded as the doer of a laudable and generous deed by his most Catholic Majesty of Spain, who, upon the assassin's execution, elevated his family to a place among the landed aristocracy? Is that the honest way of teaching history? Is it honest and is it right to represent William the Silent — " the only ruler in the world's history," as says an English writer, " who may fairly be compared with Washington " — as an "ambitious mover of rebellion," who was "in turn, as best suited his policy, Lutheran, Catholic and Calvinist?" Prove to us, Father Metcalf and gentlemen, that you are in earnest in your scrupulous anxiety for honest history, by sweeping out of your schools the books which swarm with things like these — the pages are all at your service — and then we shall be readier to believe that it is as historical scholars and not as Catholic partisans that you desire to correct Swinton's record of the abuses which provoked the Reformation. Meantime, it is all a mournful and farcical straining at gnats and swallowing camels.

I have too much respect for multitudes of my Catholic fellow-citizens of Boston to believe that they approve of this strong sectarian teaching in the parochial schools, or that they will long continue to approve it when they carefully consider it. It has now become their duty to consider it. It is now their duty to ask whither they are being led, and to refuse their support and to refuse their sanction to any institutions which are nurseries of prejudice, of slander and of mischievous falsehoods. Let the reform begin among themselves. Let the thoughtful Catholic citizens of Boston read these books; let them read this history of Gazeau's; let them read this book of Bishop Gilmour's; and if they do not instantly demand more radical expurgation than any of them have ever demanded for Mr. Swinton's book, then they are not the kind of men that I believe they are, and may God have mercy on their souls.

The Catholics among us — still the vast majority — who are the warm friends of the public school, and who dislike this system which it is now sought to foist upon them, should know that these very text-books are made weapons wherewith to attack the public school. "He held that Catholic schools are scarcely less important to the progress of religion than churches," it is approvingly told of one of the bishops, in this reader, "since, if we permit our children to be educated in the public schools, their faith, if not destroyed, will be undermined; and he strove in every way to fully arouse the Catholic mind to what he considered to be the greatest danger to the progress of the Church in the United States." My Catholic brother, you should warn these men that if the public school, if free and impartial education, simple knowledge, is the greatest danger to the Church, if the Church cannot maintain itself by the simple "appeal to reason" of which Bishop Gilmour tells, cannot hold its own in a fair field, then indeed it is in a bad way.

But it may be urged that this is all nobody's business. The Catholic priest may say that he has nothing to say about any books used in any Protestant private school, and that people have a right to do what they please in their own affairs. My good friend, that argument is quite out of date. You are a hundred years behind the times when you say that. You shall go to school to my friend's five-years-old boy, if you have not got beyond that. "Let Jack alone," Will said to Dick, who was quarreling with Jack about his sled; "the sled is his, and he has a right to do whatever he will with his own." "No,

sir," retorted Dick, firmly, "he has not a right to do whatever
he will with his own ; he only has a right to do what is
right with his own." It is not our policy in this republic to
foolishly or hastily or oppressively meddle with any society or
with any man. There will never be any interference with any
man who, for religious reasons or any other, chooses to educate
his children otherwhere than in the public schools, so long as
that education is done in any just, proper and respectable way.
But our people do not recognize the right of anybody to do
whatever he pleases with his own. The interests of the State
are paramount to the caprice of any man or any body of men ;
the whole community is under sacred obligations to each child
born into it, and every one of us is on his good behavior. There
is no society among us whose affairs are or can be simply its
own affairs ; and if rank abuses or the teaching of palpable and
baneful untruths become common and regular in any private
school in Boston, whether on Moon Street or Chestnut Street
or Marlborough Street, then it is inevitable that sooner or later
there shall be such State supervision as shall stop it.

With reference to the present stress, men ask, and women,
What shall we do ? Well, I should say, in the first place, that
anything that anybody "does" in a fever is not worth the doing.
Let fever on the school question, I should say, stop in Boston,
and stop now. There is no crack of doom in hearing. The
public schools of Boston are in no danger if every man on the
School Board is a Roman Catholic next year and the year after.
Their interests are endangered if injustice is done, in their
management, to any man or to any church. And injustice
would be done if all should be insisted on which, by a strict
construction, may be due. Men talk of making the reinstate-
ment of Swinton's book in the schools a test in this conflict.
They would know, were they good generals, that, whoever is to
blame for it, that position is lost. I do not want to see it regained on the present basis of intelligence or in the spirit in
which alone it would be regained. And, if you are Protestants,
and if you choose to look upon this as a campaign, then remember that you belong to the town of Sam Adams, and that the

motto of that prince of tacticians was, "Always keep the enemy in the wrong." Your cause will never suffer from your generosity; it may suffer much from envy, hatred or malice or any uncharitableness. Insist on nothing that the great majority do not concede to be fair, and keep on telling the truth as fast as you are quite sure you know what the truth is.

Upon you, the women of Boston, there has suddenly come a very great and a remarkable responsibility. You are suddenly called upon to exercise political power under the most trying of conditions, when politics is mixed with religious animosities and the most violent appeals are made to prejudice and passion. The enemies of woman suffrage will be quick to point to every extravagance and indiscretion on your part, in the brave performance of a trying duty, as an impeachment of your cause as women. That cause can only be advanced by this experience, whatever the vote may be this year or next It is not the less important that the coming vote be sober and intelligent, uninfluenced by the violent partisanship of either Protestant parson or Catholic priest. I do not say this to the women of this league — I sincerely wish that the voting of the men of Boston would be as just and careful as yours is sure to be — but I say it to the hundreds of women whom it is in your power to reach.

As concerns our School Board, I sincerely wish that sectarianism might never again be recognized in connection with it. I wish that no man might ever again submit a petition to it in his capacity as member of any Evangelical Alliance but only in his capacity as a citizen of Boston. I wish that none of us might speak of any church having a "fair share" of representation on the Board. No church, Catholic or Presbyterian or Unitarian, is entitled to any "share" of the School Board, or to be thought of in connection with the School Board The School Board is not an ecclesiastical tribunal; it is not, as it has sometimes become in some cities in our country, a way station for ward politicians on their way to the Common Council it is the body charged with the education of the children of Boston. The direction of the public schools of Boston is a work as momentous as the direction of Harvard University. More money is concerned, the interests are as high. The School Board of the City of Boston should be a body as dignified, as responsible and as well trained as the overseers of Harvard University, composed of those men among us who are actuated by the loftiest public spirit and who know most about education. The history of Boston has been such — this is no reflection upon anybody, I do not state it as anything that any cultivated Catholic can resent, there are cities where it would not be true — that the proportion today of our better educated men who are Catholics is but small. Leaving out the question of sectarianism therefore, which always should be left out, I should expect that the large majority of the Boston School Board today would not be Catholics. Such a condition would be only proper. Yet Boston has very many Roman Catholics as worthy as any of her citizens of place on the School Board. No vote should ever be withheld from any because he is a Catholic. But let us hear no more about any church being entitled to a "fair share " of representation.

I have endeavored, ladies and gentlemen, to give you the most serious word which it is in my power to give on this exciting and important question. I have spoken more severely upon some points than it is my wont to speak; but there are matters upon which "plain truth is all the kindness that will last." I am less anxious to help any side in this immediate controversy than to improve the occasion to direct more careful attention to facts which will remain to affect tomorrow's controversy also. I cannot doubt that out of all this commotion will come increased devotion on the part of every good citizen to the great interests of the public school. Despite all criticism and all grounds for criticism, our public schools are doubtless better today than they ever were before. Let us resolve, every one of us, to make them better still.

I wish for one that we might see a decadence of private schools altogether. No one could speak more warmly than I of many of the private schools of Boston and of other cities, and the private school doubtless has a certain proper place, but

I do not wish to see the system grow. I have little more
affection for the Protestant private school than for the Catholic. The private school tends to create and encourage class
distinctions, it draws away the personal interest of many
parents, men whose interest we most need, from the public
school, it does not make for sturdiness, it does not make for
democracy, it does not make for public spirit. I wish that
every one of you might read — it has been published, and
you all can read it — the noble address of Phillips Brooks
at the two hundred and fiftieth anniversary of the founding
of our Latin School, and let it help you realize that it is
the public school and the public school alone in which and
by which our boys and girls can be trained to that public
spirit and that free and equal democratic feeling which are the
fundamental requirements in our democratic State. And then
— this is my last word — go back two thousand years and
more, open Aristotle's *Politics* to his chapters upon public
and private schools, upon education in relation to the State.
Read those pages well, for nothing wiser has been written from
that time to this, and learn from that old "heathen" that no
polity, no State, can long endure, that none is safe, whose
children are not educated in hearty sympathy with its institutions and with its own fundamental principles. Ponder the
pages of that old "heathen" well, ladies and gentlemen, for they
contain the truth necessary for these times.

Martin Luther:

A STUDY OF REFORMATION. By Edwin D. Mead. Cloth, 12mo, 194 pages. Price, $1.25. For sale by all booksellers. Sent, postpaid, on receipt of price, by the publisher, George H. Ellis, Boston.

An essay upon the significant phases of Luther's life and work, with special reference to present problems of reform; discussing the principles of Individualism and Rationalism for which Luther stood, and the Libertinism, the Old Orthodoxy and the New Orthodoxy with which he came into conflict. First published on the occasion of the Luther quadricentenary, this work is less a historical study than a tract for the times; and as such it is chiefly commended to the attention of those who are interested in the questions which now agitate our churches and general religious circles.

———————

We recall the sensation of pleasure with which, a year or two ago, we turned from the swarm of bulky Carlyle books of high and low degree to Mr. Mead's discriminating and compact little volume on *The Philosophy of Carlyle*. With a similar sensation we welcome, among the host of books, reviews and magazine articles on Luther and his times, Mr. Mead's *Martin Luther, a Study of Reformation*. It has the same firm literary qualities as the study of Carlyle. The book exhibits that combination of conciseness of statement with breadth of view which ought to be a good deal more common than it is, since, as a rule, it is only the author who has half-mastered his subject who needs reams of paper to express himself. One cannot read the first chapter without perceiving that here is a book which is worth while.— *Boston Journal*.

Mr. Mead's monograph on Luther is a bright and panoramic view of the movement of the Reformation, written somewhat in the fashion of Carlyle's *French Revolution*, and intended to exhibit Luther as he lived, battled, thought and served. It lets in light which, if not new, has not been sufficiently used by others. What is most marked in Mr. Mead's work, and it is perhaps more manifest in this volume than in anything he has heretofore written, is a certain mental freedom, a grasp of the right conditions of his subject, an outlook upon the world from a fresh point of view. After all that has been written about Luther, Mr. Mead gives us better insight into the world in which he lived than any of the writers who have helped to celebrate his 400th birthday.— *Boston Advertiser*.

Mr. Mead's plan is to set forth the conditions of life in the sixteenth century, the state of society, the way things were looked at on both the Protestant and Catholic sides. He presumes a familiarity with the history, at least with its outlines, but goes beyond that, and seeks to revive Luther's points in theology, his quaint notions, his broad and generous humanity, the things in which, by his age and nationality, he was a different man from the American. These features distinguish Mr. Mead's work from that of other writers, and give it a zest of its own. He brings Luther nearer to ourselves than Köstlin does, or than any of the recent anniversary orators did. He does more. He interprets Luther to the modern mind and spirit. He discusses Luther for his time, but with the breadth and vigor of a thoroughly modern man.— *Boston Herald*.

The word here spoken by Mr. Mead is one much needed at the close of the debate called forth by the Luther anniversaries. These chapters tell us, what is well worth hearing, that the Roman answer to the great demonstration of enthusiasm for Luther's memory has been nothing more than a warming over of the ancient dish of absurd and monstrous calumnies which, from Luther's time until now, has been served up for the satisfying of the faithful. It is a good service to point out, as Mr. Mead has done, that what seems to many the failure of Protestantism is nothing more than the failure of certain schemes and certain combinations going under the name of Protestant; while the real thing, the spirit of Protestantism, is moving on in other forms to ever-new victories. Mr. Mead's hero-worship is far from that blind reverence which sees only good in its object. He recognizes Luther's faults and dwells upon them. Only he insists that these faults, which have been seized upon as a reproach to the great cause, had really to do with the cause only in so far as they helped to make up the mighty individuality of the man.— *The Nation*.

Those of us who remember that, when the market seemed burdened with books about Carlyle, it was the little volume by Mr. Mead that was welcomed here and in England as the word that helped most of all to clear the atmosphere, and show the rugged Scotchman in his true position, are prepared to expect help from the same pen in gaining a true conception of the word and work of the great German. This book is all one great sermon, ending, in the good old style, with an improvement suited to our present time and situation; only it must be understood that it is a sermon without a dull line.— *Chicago Tribune*.

www.ingramcontent.com/pod-product-compliance
Lightning Source LLC
Chambersburg PA
CBHW021553270326
41931CB00009B/1189